Ecosystems

by Helen N. George

PEARSON
Scott Foresman

What are the parts of ecosystems?

What a System Is

A system has parts. These parts work together to do a job. A system can have living and nonliving parts. Every part of a system is important. The system will not work as well if any part is damaged or missing.

A bicycle is a simple system. The frame, handlebars, and the rider all work together.

Most ecosystems have inputs. Inputs are things coming into the system. They also have outputs. Outputs are things leaving the system. The activity of the rider is an input of a bicycle system. The dust from the tires is one output.

Ecosystems

An **ecosystem** is all of the living and nonliving things in an environment and the ways in which they interact. An ecosystem can be as large as a desert. It can be as small as a rotting cactus.

The living things in an ecosystem are animals, plants, fungi, protists, and bacteria. The nonliving things in an ecosystem are air, water, soil, sunlight, climate, and landforms. The living and nonliving parts work together.

Kinds of Ecosystems

The needs of an organism must be met in its environment. Some plants and animals will survive in the environment better than others will. Some will not survive at all. Soil and climate affect which plants and animals will do well in an area. Desert plants and animals have adaptations to help them live in a dry environment. The giant saguaro cactus can fill up with water. It can store this water until the next rainfall.

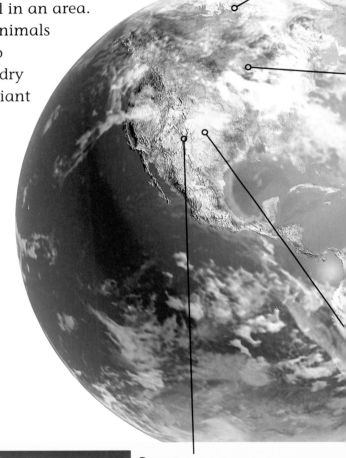

Desert
A desert is the driest ecosystem. Plants and animals adapt to live with little water. Some desert organisms are roadrunners, coyotes, shrubs, and cactuses.

Tundra

A tundra is cold and dry. The ground under the surface is frozen all year long. Some grasses can grow. Trees cannot grow. Caribou and arctic foxes do well during the spring and summer.

Forest

Forests get more rain than grasslands do. Forests have many animals, trees, and wildflowers. Some forest animals are squirrels, raccoons, deer, and foxes.

Tropical Rain Forest

A rain forest is always wet. There are many species of plants and animals in the rain forest. Colorful birds live there. Beautiful flowers live there.

Grasslands

Grasslands are covered with grass. They have moderate rainfall. Bison, prairie chickens, and grasshoppers are found in North American grasslands.

Organisms and Their Environment

A **population** is one species of organisms that live in a part of an ecosystem. Prairie dogs make up one animal population in a desert. Barrel cactuses make up a plant population in the desert. The size of a population depends on how much water, food, and space there is.

Different populations can live together in the same area. They make up a **community.** All the organisms found in a desert ecosystem are a community.

A habitat is where an organism lives within an ecosystem. The habitat of the Gambel's quail is near shrubs in the Sonoran desert. It can hide from predators there. Everything an organism needs to survive is found in its habitat.

Special Roles

Every organism has a job to do in its habitat. This is its **niche.** A niche includes the food the organism eats, how it gets its food, and which other species use the organism for food.

Every population in a habitat has a different niche. Hummingbirds and roadrunners share a desert habitat. They have different niches. The Lucifer hummingbird eats small insects, spiders, and nectar from plants. It hides from its enemies, such as the roadrunner, by sitting on tall plants. The roadrunner's niche is to hunt scorpions, lizards, and snakes. It runs away from enemies, such as the coyote.

7

How does energy flow in ecosystems?

Energy in Plants and Animals

The main energy source for life on Earth is the Sun. During photosynthesis, green plants change energy from the Sun into chemical energy. This chemical energy keeps the plant alive. Plants are called producers. They make, or produce, their own food.

Many organisms cannot make their own food. They must eat other organisms. Consumers are organisms that eat other living things. **Herbivores** are consumers that get energy by eating plants. **Carnivores** are consumers that eat animals. **Omnivores** eat both plants and animals. Consumers that eat dead plants and animals are scavengers. Some scavengers are carnivores.

Mountain lion—carnivore

Organisms may have different adaptations to help them survive in their niche. Some carnivores, such as mountain lions, have claws to help them catch their prey. Mountain lions also have sharp teeth for eating the prey. Herbivores such as deer do not need to catch their food. They have teeth for tearing leaves off plants. Some herbivores have stomachs with four parts to help them digest their food. Scavengers, such as turkey vultures, tear meat with their sharp beaks.

Bighorn sheep—herbivore

Coati—omnivore

A Food Chain

The energy that producers store moves through a food chain. This happens when organisms eat and are eaten.

Food chains start with energy from the Sun. The energy moves to producers. Energy moves through a food chain. It flows from the "eaten" to the "eater." Arrows in a food chain diagram show how the energy is moving.

A desert ecosystem has food chains. In one food chain the prickly pear cactus is a producer. It takes in energy from the Sun. An omnivore such as the collared peccary eats the prickly pear cactus. The collared peccary takes in energy that was stored in the cactus. A predator such as the coyote hunts the collared peccary. Then the coyote takes in energy from the collared peccary, which got energy from the cactus.

Collared peccary—omnivore

Small Things That Make a Big Difference

What if an ecosystem had only producers and consumers? One day the nutrients in the soil would be used up. The plants would die. Then there would be nothing for the herbivores to eat. Nutrients and minerals must be put back.

Decomposers are organisms that eat the waste and remains of dead plants and animals. Food energy is stored in these remains. Insects, fungi, and some bacteria are decomposers.

Mushrooms are fungi. They are decomposers.

Decomposers break down the plant and animal remains into minerals and nutrients. These minerals and nutrients go back into the water, air, and soil. Living plants take them in. Animals take in these minerals and nutrients when they eat the plants.

Anything that affects decomposers will affect the soil in an ecosystem. It can also affect producers and consumers in that ecosystem.

Decomposers are breaking down this cactus.

A Food Web

One food source can be part of several food chains. A food web is a system of overlapping food chains. Energy moves in many directions in a food web.

Producers and consumers may be eaten by many different organisms. Predators often eat more than one kind of prey.

Black-tailed jackrabbit

Prickly pear cactus

Collared peccary

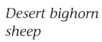

Desert bighorn sheep

In a desert ecosystem, the coyote and the mountain lion compete for black-tailed jackrabbits and Gambel's quails. They eat collared peccaries too.

Look at this food web. Did you notice that roadrunners eat rattlesnakes? A roadrunner can run 25 kilometers per hour. It is one of the few animals that can catch a rattlesnake.

A food web can change any time the size of a population changes. Hunting, storms, pollution, and disease can also change a food web.

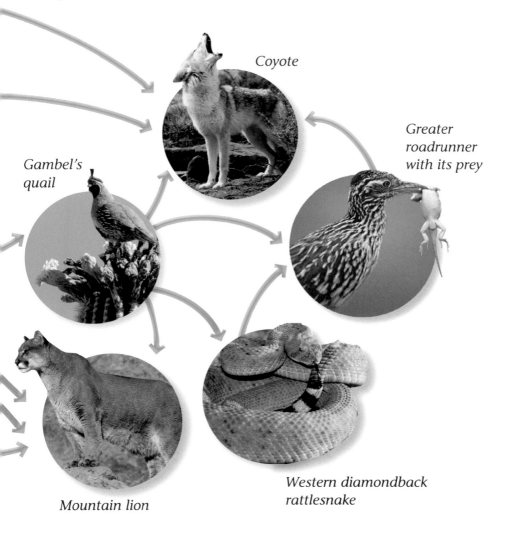

Coyote

Greater roadrunner with its prey

Gambel's quail

Mountain lion

Western diamondback rattlesnake

How does matter flow in ecosystems?

Water Ecosystems

Almost three-fourths of the surface of Earth is covered with water. Many organisms live in water ecosystems. Some organisms live in the salt water of ocean ecosystems. Other organisms live in fresh water.

Wetlands are another kind of water ecosystem. In wetlands, water is covering the soil or is near the top of the soil. Swamps are wetlands that are wet all year. The Okefenokee Swamp in southern Georgia and northern Florida has many producers.

Okefenokee Swamp

One large producer in the Okefenokee Swamp is the bald cypress tree. This tree has needlelike leaves. The bottom of the bald cypress tree is very wide. Parts that grow from the roots and stick out of the water look like "knees." Some bald cypress trees grow more than 30 meters (100 feet) tall.

Single-celled algae are small producers in the Okefenokee Swamp. These plantlike protists carry out photosynthesis. This makes them producers.

Matter and energy move through an ecosystem. Plants take in nutrients from the soil. They also take in gases from the air. Herbivores eat plants to get the matter and energy they need. The matter and energy pass to carnivores that eat the herbivores.

Algae have only one cell. They are producers.

17

How Matter Flows Through A Food Web

A food chain shows how matter and energy flow through an ecosystem. Producers and consumers can be part of more than one food chain. The overlapping food chains are a food web.

Single-celled algae take in sunlight and matter from their environment. Zooplankton feed on algae. Freshwater snails also feed on algae. These snails are consumers. They are prey of the great blue heron. The blue-spotted sunfish lives near beds of algae. It eats zooplankton and other small invertebrates.

Freshwater snail

Algae

Blue-spotted sunfish

Zooplankton

Sandhill crane

Osprey

Great blue heron

The sandhill crane is an omnivore. It eats many different things. It eats seeds, berries, invertebrates, reptiles, and fish. The great blue heron eats mollusks and amphibians. It stabs its prey with its beak and swallows it whole. The osprey is a carnivore. It eats mostly fish. Sometimes it eats snakes and amphibians.

Look at this swamp food web. Follow the arrows to see how energy flows to and from all the different organisms.

Decay in Ecosystems

All living things will die and rot, or decay. Ecosystems need decay. Without decay, wastes and dead organisms would build up and get in the way of living organisms.

Decay begins when scavengers eat parts of dead organisms. Decomposers such as bacteria and fungi break down the dead organisms. This returns nutrients and minerals to the ecosystem.

Rate of Decay

An organism decays more slowly in colder temperatures. It decays faster in warmer temperatures.

Oxygen also speeds decay. Some bacteria and fungi need oxygen to grow and live. That is why you keep food covered.

Moisture also affects decay. Moisture makes many decomposers grow better and work faster.

Nonliving objects decay much more slowly than objects that used to be alive. Decomposers will break down a dead insect faster than a pebble.

Oxygen helps organisms break down food. Organisms get energy from food. They put carbon dioxide into the air or water.

Plants take in carbon dioxide from the air or water. They also put oxygen back into the air.

Carbon dioxide is part of the decay process. It is put into the air when decomposers break down dead organisms.

Ecosystems have many living and nonliving parts. The parts work together. All the organisms in an ecosystem have needs. Organisms are adapted to survive in their ecosystem. A cactus, for example, is adapted to the dry desert. Many populations of organisms work together to make up a community. Every organism has a niche, or job, within its habitat.

Living things need energy. A food chain shows how energy moves from one organism to another. Food chains always begin with energy from the Sun. Sometimes several food chains overlap and form a food web.

Living things also need matter. They need minerals, oxygen, and carbon dioxide. Matter flows through a food web in the same way that energy does. In any ecosystem, decay is needed. Decay returns minerals and nutrients to the soil.

Glossary

carnivores   consumers that get energy from eating animals

community   different populations that work together in an ecosystem

decomposers   organisms that break down dead organisms

ecosystem   all the living and nonliving things in an environment and how they interact

herbivores   consumers that get energy from eating plants

niche   the special role or job of an organism in its habitat

omnivores   consumers that get energy from eating both animals and plants

population   all the organisms of one species in an ecosystem